KT-470-316

Withdrawn From Stock
Dublin Public Libraries

READY-TO-EAT
VEGETARIAN
PARTY FOOD
Delectable vegetable-forward bites for entertaining

Leabharlanna Poibli Chathair Baile Átha Cliath
Dublin City Public Libraries

Jessica Oldfield

Photography by Beatriz da Costa

hardie grant books

CHOPPING BOARD

SHARP KNIFE

LARGE HEAVY-BASED FRYING PAN

SLOTTED SPOON

TONGS

THE ONLY TOOLS YOU NEED
FOR THIS BOOK

WOK

CONTENTS

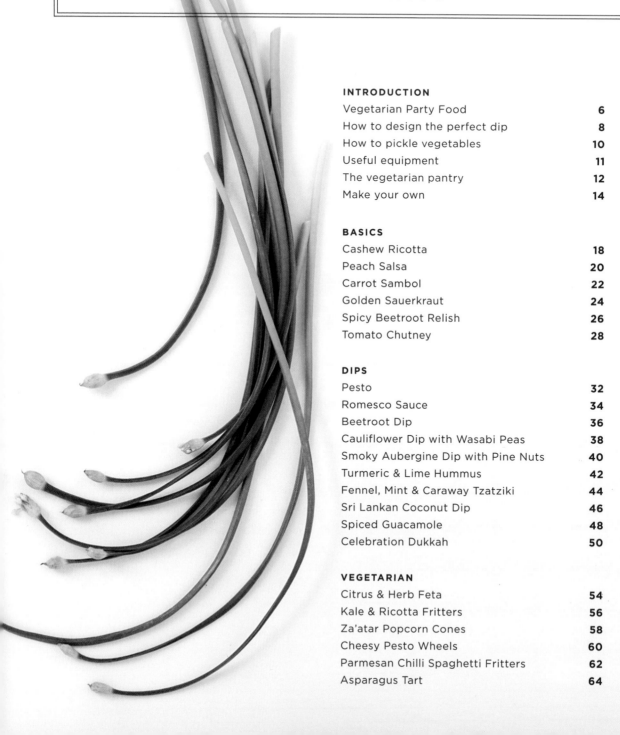

VEGETARIAN PARTY FOOD

Honing the art of gatherings is simple: bring together good food and good friends. This philosophy of effortless get-togethers, whether impromptu or planned, underpins the food in this book. The recipes are simple, quick to make and delicious. There is a variety of snacks, starters and stylish bites to pass round or fill the table for a colourful feast, all inspired with a world-food twist: vibrant beetroot hasselbacks stuffed with citrus and herb feta; spanikopita cigars of ricotta and spinach wrapped in filo pastry; crispy paneer dumplings drizzled with green chilli oil; or a bowl of zesty turmeric and lime hummus.

Cooking memorable food to share doesn't need to be stressful or complicated. The key is quality ingredients and organisation. Over the next few pages there's a useful equipment list and essential ingredients to get your pantry stocked for party season. If hosting an event is something you have always wanted to try, here are a few helpful tips to ensure your next soirée is smooth sailing.

First, plan your menu, then confirm your guest list and calculate how much food you will need. You may need to multiply recipes to ensure adequate servings. Compile as many recipes from this book as you want but make sure your menu is balanced and practical, and consider how much time you have to prepare.

6

Next, write a shopping list. Consolidate all ingredients needed into one list. If doing one shop isn't practical, buy non-perishable items ahead and fresh ingredients the day before the event.

It's useful to create prep lists. Read the recipes and create lists according to what can be prepped when. For example, a day-before prep list, an event-day prep list, an hour-before serving prep list, etc. Tasks such as marinating are best done the day before to improve flavour.

Before you start preparing make sure you have all the equipment you'll need to cook and serve each menu item. Refer to the useful equipment list on page 11, then begin working through prep lists in order. Ensure foods are stored in sealed containers to maintain freshness.

Finally, be thoughtful when plating each dish. Consider height and colour and select serving boards and plates that complement or contrast with the colours in the dish. Although most ingredients can be prepared in advance, complete final assembly just before serving and double check seasoning.

HOW TO DESIGN THE PERFECT DIP

Homemade dips are easy, delicious and often healthier than the shop-bought varieties.
Get creative with this simple 'food map', designed to help you whip up a crowd pleaser
using versatile ingredients

1.

CHOOSE A MAIN VEGETABLE (200–250 G/7–9 OZ)

Select from: **beetroot (beets)** – cooked, skin removed, roughly chopped; **(bell) pepper** – cooked, roughly chopped; **courgette (zucchini)** – cooked or raw, roughly chopped; **aubergine (eggplant)** – cooked, skin removed, roughly chopped; **pumpkin** – cooked, skin and seeds removed, roughly chopped; **mushrooms** – cooked, stems removed, roughly chopped; **baby spinach** – cooked or raw; **sweet potato** – cooked, skin removed, roughly chopped.

2.

CHOOSE BACK-UP BEANS OR PULSES (300–400 G/ 10½–14 OZ)

Pick from: **red lentils** – cooked or sprouted; **mung beans** – cooked or sprouted; **chickpeas (garbanzo beans)** – cooked, skins removed; **puy lentils** – cooked or sprouted; butter beans – cooked; **broad (fava) beans** – podded, cooked.

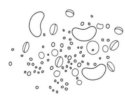

3.

ADD RICHNESS (3–4 TABLESPOONS)

Choose from: **Greek or natural yoghurt; coconut yoghurt; tahini; smashed avocado flesh; extra-virgin olive oil; cold-pressed avocado oil; feta; goat's cheese.**

4.

CHOOSE A KEY FLAVOUR

Pick from:
1–2 tablespoons **harissa paste**; 1–2 teaspoons **ground sumac**;
1 **chipotle pepper in adobo**, deseeded and crushed into a paste;
1–2 teaspoons **ground cumin**, dry-fried;
1–2 cloves **garlic**, crushed; juice and finely grated zest of 1–2 **lemons**.

5.

CHOOSE A BACK-UP FLAVOUR

Go for: a handful of **mint leaves**; a handful of **basil leaves**; 1 **red or green chilli**, deseeded and finely chopped; a handful of **currants**; 1–2 teaspoons **ground cinnamon**; juice and finely grated zest of 1 **orange**; juice and finely grated zest 1–2 **limes**.

6.

CHOOSE A CRUNCHY TOPPING (A GENEROUS HANDFUL PLUS EXTRA TO REPLENISH)

Decide on: **dukkah**; **sage leaves**, fried until crisp; **almonds**, toasted; **pine nuts**, lightly toasted; **fennel seeds**, lightly toasted; **cumin seeds**, lightly toasted; **pumpkin seeds**, toasted and salted; **sunflower seeds**, toasted and salted; **fried shallots**; **mixed olives**, pitted and sliced; seedless **red or green grapes**, sliced.

7.

MAKE YOUR DIP

Choose one (or more) ingredient under each heading (except toppings), and combine in a food processor. Add a generous pinch of salt and pepper, then mix until smooth or a desired consistency is achieved. Transfer to your favourite wide-rimmed, shallow serving bowl, drizzle with extra oil and sprinkle over one or more crunchy toppings of choice. Serve with crackers, warm or toasted bread, raw and roasted vegetables.

HOW TO PICKLE VEGETABLES

Fermented vegetables taste delicious and are also good for your digestion. You can pickle just about any vegetable and flavour it with any herbs and spices. They make a great topping for finger food.

STERILISE JARS

Wash jars and lids in hot soapy water, then while still wet, place them upside down on an ovenproof tray. Pop the tray of clean, wet jars and lids into an oven preheated to 160–180°C (325–350°F/Gas 3–4) for 15 minutes.

PREPARE VEGETABLES

You will need 600 g (1 lb 5 oz) of vegetables of your choice. Experiment by mixing varieties. Chop or slice large vegetables, keep baby varieties whole. Choose seasonal vegetables, organic if possible.

MAKE PICKLING BRINE

Pickling brine is salt dissolved in water at a ratio of 5 per cent salt to the volume of water. Always use filtered, not tap water. Combine 4 teaspoons salt into 400 ml (14 fl oz) water, making sure all the salt is dissolved.

CHOOSE FLAVOURINGS

Select your choice of herbs and spices, around 1 tablespoon of each. Again experiment with different combinations – dill and black pepper or tarragon and red chilli are delicious combinations to try.

ASSEMBLE

Put all the spices and herbs in the jar, then add the vegetables. They should be snug. Pour in the brine, filling to the brim. Make sure all the vegetables are below the surface of the brine. Sit a lid over the top of the jar, but don't tighten. Place small cloth on top and secure with a rubber band.

FERMENT

Sit the jar on a plate and leave for 5–7 days at room temperature until the colour of the vegetable turns from bright to pale. You may see a fine, white mould form on the surface, just wash it off before putting the pickles in the refrigerator. The pickles should smell good and taste crunchy. If not, leave for a few more days. Chill for up to one year.

USEFUL EQUIPMENT

You don't need any special equipment when making the dishes in this book, but these extra tools will help you prepare and make your dishes even quicker and easier.

This is useful but not essential as it allows you to blitz large amounts of food quickly and the interchangeable attachments allow you to chop, shred, slice and dice vegetables quickly.

FOOD PROCESSOR

It is a good idea to have a selection of different-sized serving platters and boards and serving bowls in contrasting styles and colours. Use small bowls for dipping sauces.

SERVING PLATTERS/ DIPPING BOWLS

This tool is not essential but it makes slicing vegetables and fruit very thinly and evenly a lot easier. The blades are very sharp so use with care and make sure to slice away from you.

MANDOLINE SLICER

All kitchens should have a mortar and pestle as they are convenient to use. They are great for crushing and grinding spices, fresh herb leaves and for making pastes.

MORTAR AND PESTLE

This is a useful tool to have in the kitchen as it's versatile, easy to use and small enough to store anywhere. You can quickly whizz up pesto, salsas or make a sauce in a matter of minutes.

STICK BLENDER

THE VEGETARIAN PANTRY

Keep your pantry well stocked and flavourful snacks and sharing food will be only a moment's preparation away. Always buy the best quality you can afford, and organic where possible.

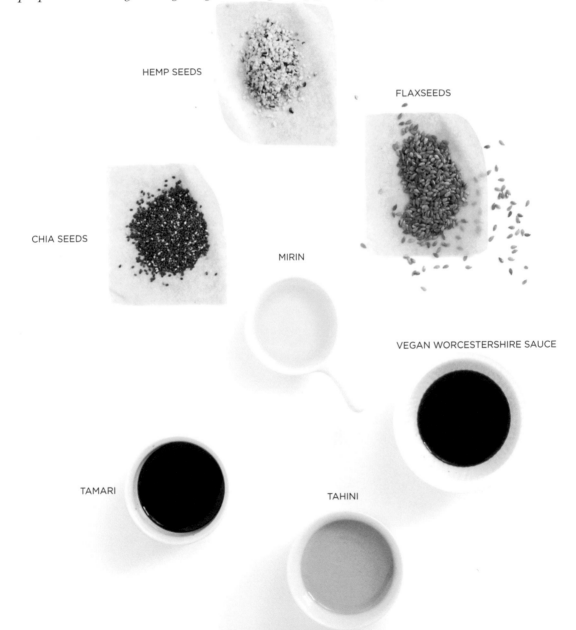

HEMP SEEDS

FLAXSEEDS

CHIA SEEDS

MIRIN

VEGAN WORCESTERSHIRE SAUCE

TAMARI

TAHINI

12

ZA'ATAR SPICE BLEND

TAMARIND PASTE

CORIANDER
SEEDS

CHILLI POWDER

POMEGRANATE MOLASSES

PAPRIKA

CUMIN SEEDS

GROUND
TURMERIC

BLACK & WHITE
SESAME SEEDS

NORI SEAWEED
SHEETS

WHITE MISO PASTE

FENNEL SEEDS

TABASCO SAUCE

13

ROASTED GARLIC DRESSING

makes about 300 ml (10 fl oz/1¼ cups)

2 heads of garlic, roasted whole
250 g (9 oz) plain Greek yoghurt
½ teaspoon apple cider vinegar
2 tablespoons extra-virgin olive oil
¼ teaspoon salt

Squeeze the roasted garlic from the skins into a bowl and discard the skins. Add all other ingredients and blend with a stick blender until smooth. Store in airtight container in the refrigerator for 3–5 days.

GREEN CHILLI OIL

makes 500 ml (17 fl oz/2 cups)

8 green chillies (120 g/4¼ oz), stalks removed
    and roughly chopped
500 ml (17 fl oz/2 cups) extra-virgin olive oil

Bruise the chillies in a mortar and pestle, then transfer to a 500 ml (17 fl oz/2 cup) sterilised jar and cover with the oil. The oil will intensify in flavour over time. Store sealed in the refrigerator for up to 6 months.

CUCUMBER PICKLE

makes about 800 g (1¾ lb)

800 g (1¾ lb) small mixed cucumbers, sliced into 5 mm (¼ in) rounds

500 ml (17 fl oz/2 cups) white vinegar

110 g (3¾ oz) white caster (superfine) sugar

small bunch of dill (30 g/1 oz), stalks trimmed

1 tablespoon salt

1 cabbage leaf

Heat the vinegar, sugar, salt and 250 ml (1 cup) water until the sugar dissolves, then bring to the boil. Layer the dill and cucumber in jar, then pour over the brine. Place the cabbage leaf on top and press down, seal and chill for 2 weeks.

15

VEGAN MAYO

makes about 250 g (9 oz)

300 g (10½ oz) silken tofu

1½ teaspoons Dijon mustard

juice of 1 lime

½ teaspoon salt

2 tablespoons extra-virgin olive oil

Place the tofu in a sieve, cover with a kitchen towel and sit over a bowl. Place a heavy object on top and compress the tofu for 15 minutes. Discard the drained liquid. Blend the tofu and all the other ingredients until smooth. Store in the refrigerator for up to 1 week.

BASICS
made simple

Master these six basic recipes as part of your on-hand staples
to add a punch of flavour and satisfying texture to your next
bite-sized menu.

CASHEW RICOTTA

Preparation: 25 minutes
Chilling: 1 hour

makes 300 g (10½ oz)

250 g (9 oz) cashews, soaked in warm water for 20 minutes
squeeze of lemon juice
1 teaspoon nutritional yeast flakes
1 teaspoon salt

method

Blend all the ingredients in a food processor until smooth. Roll the cheese into a log shape or ball using a piece of muslin. Place in the refrigerator for 1 hour to chill and set. Store in an airtight container in the refrigerator for 1–2 weeks. It will keep in the freezer for up to a month.

PEACH SALSA

Preparation: 15 minutes

serves 4

4 ripe yellow peaches (580 g/20 ½ oz), halved,
   stoned, and grilled (broiled)
1 avocado, peeled, pitted and roughly chopped
1 small red onion, finely diced
juice of 1 lime
handful of coriander (cilantro) leaves, plus extra to
   garnish
¼ teaspoon Tabasco sauce

method

Chop the grilled peaches into small pieces and combine with the remaining ingredients.
Season with salt to taste and mix well. Garnish with more coriander.

CARROT SAMBOL

Preparation: 10 minutes
Cooking: 5 minutes

22

makes about 200 g (7 oz)

40 g (1½ oz) desiccated (dried shredded) coconut
10 fresh curry leaves
2 carrots, finely shredded
½ small red onion, finely sliced
1 green chilli, finely sliced
juice of 1 lime
½ teaspoon salt

method

Preheat the oven to 140°C (275°F/Gas 1). Place the coconut and curry leaves on a baking paper-lined baking tray (sheet) and bake for 5 minutes until warm, but not coloured. Transfer to a bowl and combine with the remaining ingredients.

GOLDEN SAUERKRAUT

Preparation: 20 minutes
Fermenting: 5–7 days

24

*makes about
1 kg (2¼ lbs)*

400 g (14 oz) golden
   beetroot (beets),
   peeled and finely shredded
1 tablespoon cumin seeds
1 tablespoon cracked black pepper
1 tablespoon fennel seeds
1 tablespoon ground turmeric
½ green cabbage (about 600 g/1 lb 5 oz), core removed and
   finely shredded (reserve some outer layers of the cabbage
   for packaging on top to prevent oxidisation)
1 tablespoon salt

method

Place all the ingredients in a large bowl. Use your hands (wear gloves to avoid staining your hands) to massage the vegetables until the juices are released, about 10 minutes. Pack the vegetables tightly into a sterilised jar, pressing them down so that the liquid rises above the vegetables and air bubbles are released. Leave some space at top to place a whole folded cabbage leaf. Close and seal with an airtight lid. Leave to ferment at room temperature, but out of direct sunlight for 5–7 days. Remove the cabbage leaf and chill for up to 6 months.

SPICY BEETROOT RELISH

Preparation: 15 minutes
Cooking: 10 minutes

makes about 500 g (2 lb 2 oz)

3 tablespoons coconut oil
6 fresh curry leaves
1 long green chilli, finely chopped
2 medium beetroot (beets) (about 500 g/2 lb 2 oz), peeled
and finely shredded
2 tablespoons tamarind paste
salt

method

Heat the oil in a frying pan over medium–high heat and fry the curry leaves for 30 seconds. Add the chilli and cook for 1 minute. Reduce the heat to medium, add the beetroot and cook for 10 minutes. Take the pan off the heat, stir in the tamarind paste and season with salt to taste. Store in an airtight container in the refrigerator for up to a week.

TOMATO CHUTNEY

Preparation: 5 minutes
Cooking: 40 minutes

makes about 485 g (1 lb 1 oz)

500 g (1 lb 2 oz) mixed-colour cherry tomatoes, roughly chopped
250 g (9 oz) red onion, thinly sliced
80 ml (2¾ fl oz/⅓ cup) raspberry wine or red wine vinegar
½ dried anjo or habanero chilli, finely chopped
½ teaspoon salt

method

Put all the ingredients into a pan and stir well to combine. Simmer for 30–40 minutes, or until jammy. Pour into a sterilised jar, seal and store in the refrigerator for up to a week.

DIPS
made simple

Serve these dips with crackers and raw or roasted vegetables for the perfect snack to share over a drink. You can use the guide on page 8 to create your own signature flavours, if you like.

PESTO

Preparation: 10 minutes

32

makes about 250 g (9 oz)

4 tablespoons pine nuts, lightly toasted
100 g (3½ oz) basil leaves
1 tablespoon hemp seeds (optional)
finely grated zest of 1 lemon
1 tablespoon lemon juice
80 ml (2¾ fl oz/⅓ cup) extra-virgin olive oil
½ small garlic clove, peeled
¼ teaspoon salt

method

Place all the ingredients in a food processor and pulse until combined.

ROMESCO SAUCE

Preparation: 5 minutes
Cooking: 15 minutes

34

serves 4

2 red (bell) peppers, blackened over
    an open flame, peeled and deseeded
100 g (3½ oz) blanched almonds,
    toasted
1 garlic clove, peeled and crushed
1 small roma (plum) tomato, chopped
1 tablespoon raspberry wine vinegar
¼ teaspoon salt
120 ml (4 fl oz/½ cup) extra-virgin olive oil

method

Blend all the ingredients except the olive oil in a food processor until finely chopped.
Drizzle in the olive oil and pulse until combined.

BEETROOT DIP

Preparation: 10 minutes
Cooking: 25 minutes

36

makes about 500 g (1 lb 2 oz)

850 g (1 lb 14 oz) beetroot (beets), roasted,
    peeled and roughly chopped
4 teaspoons finely grated fresh horseradish
60 ml (2 fl oz/¼ cup) extra-virgin olive oil
¼ teaspoon salt
140 g (5 oz) Greek yoghurt
1½ tablespoons pomegranate molasses
½ teaspoon cumin seeds, toasted

method

Pulse the beetroot, horseradish, yoghurt, olive oil and salt in a food processor until smooth.
Transfer to a shallow, wide-rimmed bowl and dollop small spoonfuls of the yoghurt on top.
Draw a skewer through the yoghurt and beetroot to create a marbled effect. Drizzle over
the molasses and scatter with cumin seeds. Serve with crackers.

CAULIFLOWER DIP WITH WASABI PEAS

Preparation: 5 minutes
Cooking: 30 minutes

38

serves 4

4 tablespoons extra-virgin olive oil
5 garlic cloves, peeled and thinly sliced
650 g (1 lb 7 oz) cauliflower, very finely chopped
½ teaspoon salt
200 ml (7 fl oz/generous ¾ cup) coconut cream
2 tablespoons honey
1 tablespoon wasabi peas, roughly crushed

method

Heat the oil in a saucepan over medium heat and fry the garlic for a minute, or until fragrant. Add the cauliflower and salt and cook gently for 10 minutes, or until soft. Add the coconut cream, bring to the boil, then reduce the heat and simmer for 20 minutes, or until half the liquid has evaporated. Cool slightly, then purée with a stick blender until smooth. Transfer to a bowl and top with honey and wasabi peas.

SMOKY AUBERGINE DIP WITH PINE NUTS

Preparation: 25 minutes
Cooking: 5 minutes

serves 4

3 aubergines (eggplants), blackened over
   an open flame, peeled and flesh removed
small handful of mint leaves, plus extra roughly chopped to garnish
2 tablespoons extra-virgin olive oil, plus extra to garnish
1 teaspoon white miso paste
1 small garlic clove, peeled
½ teaspoon salt
45 g (1 oz) pine nuts, lightly toasted

40

method

Blitz the aubergine flesh, mint, olive oil, miso, garlic and salt together in a food processor until smooth. Transfer to a bowl and garnish with the extra olive oil and chopped mint and the pine nuts.

TURMERIC & LIME HUMMUS

Preparation: 10 minutes

42

serves 4

350 g (12 oz) cooked chickpeas (garbanzo beans), skins removed,
   plus a few extra to garnish
1 garlic clove, peeled and crushed
juice of 2 limes, plus grated zest to garnish
60 ml (2 fl oz/¼ cup) extra-virgin olive oil, plus extra to garnish
½ teaspoon ground turmeric
1 teaspoon salt

method

Blend all the ingredients in a food processor until completely smooth, adding
1–2 tablespoons water to loosen if needed. Transfer to a bowl and garnish with extra
chickpeas, a drizzle of olive oil and grated lime zest. Serve with bagel chips or crackers.

FENNEL, MINT & CARAWAY TZATZIKI

Preparation: 10 minutes

44

serves 4

250 g (9 oz) plain or Greek yoghurt
small bunch of mint, leaves picked and coarsely torn,
   plus extra to garnish
1 cucumber, deseeded and finely chopped
1 teaspoon fennel seeds, lightly toasted
1 teaspoon caraway seeds, lightly toasted
½ teaspoon salt
1 tablespoon extra-virgin olive oil

method

Combine all the ingredients except the olive oil in a bowl and mix well. Drizzle with the oil, then scatter extra mint leaves on top to garnish.

SRI LANKAN COCONUT DIP

Preparation: 5 minutes
Cooking: 5 minutes

serves 4

460 g (1 lb 2 oz) coconut yoghurt
½ teaspoon salt
juice of 2 limes
2 tablespoons coconut oil
1 teaspoon yellow mustard seeds
½ teaspoon ground turmeric
10 fresh curry leaves

method

Combine the yoghurt, salt and lime juice in a bowl. Heat the oil in a frying pan (skillet) over a medium heat for 1 minute before adding the mustard seeds. When the mustard seeds start to pop, add the turmeric and curry leaves. Once the curry leaves start to spit and sizzle, about 30 seconds, remove the pan from heat. Pour the spiced oil over the yoghurt mixture. Cover and chill until ready to serve.

SPICED GUACAMOLE

Preparation: 10 minutes

48

serves 4

4 avocados, peeled, pitted and chopped
juice of 2 limes, plus lime wedges to serve
1 teaspoon sweet paprika, plus extra to garnish (optional)
1 teaspoon habanero chilli powder
½ teaspoon ground cumin
½ teaspoon salt
bunch of coriander (cilantro), stalks finely chopped, leaves picked

method

Put all ingredients except the coriander leaves in a bowl and mix well. Top with the coriander, sprinkle with extra paprika, if liked, and serve with lime wedges.

CELEBRATION DUKKAH

Preparation: 20 minutes

makes about 200 g (7 oz)

70 g (2½ oz) hazelnuts, roasted and skins removed
70 g (2½ oz) macadamias, roasted
3 tablespoons coriander seeds, lightly toasted
1 tablespoon fennel seeds, lightly toasted
1 tablespoon cumin seeds, lightly toasted
2 tablespoons black sesame seeds, lightly toasted
½ teaspoon salt

method

Place all the ingredients in a mortar and pestle and coarsely crush. Store in an airtight container for up to a month.

VEGETARIAN
made simple

A selection of hot and cold sharing plates with influences from
Morocco, India, Italy and Thailand, these finger-licking morsels
are sure party starters for a casual picnic to a fancy function.

CITRUS & HERB FETA

Preparation: 10 minutes

54

makes about 1 kg (2 lb 2 oz)

20 black peppercorns
1 kg (2 lb 3 oz) feta, cut into 3 cm (1¼ in) cubes
bunch of dill (50 g/1¾ oz), leaves picked and finely chopped
bunch of parsley (50 g/1¾ oz), leaves and stalks roughly chopped
12 thyme sprigs
juice of 1 lemon, plus the zest pared into large strips
800 ml (28 fl oz/3½ cups) extra-virgin olive oil

method

Place the peppercorns in a large sterilised jar. Alternately layer the feta and herbs, adding lemon zest in the middle. Add the lemon juice and enough olive oil to completely cover the feta. Chill for at least a week before serving. The olive oil will solidify in the refrigerator. Leave the jar at room temperature for at least 1 hour before serving. Marinated feta will keep sealed in the refrigerator for up to 2 weeks.

KALE & RICOTTA FRITTERS

Preparation: 30 minutes
Cooking: 10 minutes

serves 4

300 g (10½ oz) kale, stems
    removed, leaves roughly torn
    and sautéed
160 g (5¾ oz) cooked millet
10 g (½ oz) mint leaves, plus
    extra to garnish
50 g (1¾ oz) ricotta
2 eggs
½ teaspoon salt
2 tablespoons coconut oil

method

Pulse all the ingredients except the oil in a food processor until just combined. Chill for 20 minutes to allow mixture to firm up. Heat the oil in a frying pan (skillet) over medium-high heat. Shape the mixture into 8–10 fritters and fry in batches until golden on both sides, about 4 minutes. Garnish with mint and serve.

ZA'ATAR POPCORN CONES

Preparation: 10 minutes

58

serves 6

2 tablespoons extra-virgin olive oil
450 g (1 lb) popped popcorn, still hot
½ teaspoon salt
2½ tablespoons za'atar
¼ teaspoon chilli powder
100 g (3½ oz) finely grated Parmesan-style cheese

method

Pour the oil over the hot popcorn and toss to coat. Mix the salt, za'atar and chilli powder together in a small bowl. Pour the spice mixture over the popcorn and toss until well combined. Serve immediately in paper cups or paper cones with grated cheese on top.

CHEESY PESTO WHEELS

Preparation: 10 minutes + Chilling: 30 minutes
Cooking: 20 minutes

60

serves 8

2 tablespoons Pesto (page 32)
1 sheet (24 x 24 cm/10 x 10 in) puff pastry, thawed
100 g (3½ oz) grated Cheddar
1 tablespoon dried cranberries, roughly chopped
1 egg, lightly beaten

method

Spread the pesto over the pastry sheet, leaving a 1 cm (½ in) border around the edge. Scatter over the cheese and cranberries. Brush the edges with the beaten egg. Starting from one side, roll up the pastry tightly to enclose the filling. Wrap the roll in cling film (plastic wrap) and chill for 30 minutes. Preheat the oven to 200°C (400°F/Gas 6). Brush the roll with egg, then cut it into 8 slices. Place each slice, cut-side up, on a baking-paper-lined tray (sheet). Bake for 20 minutes, or until golden.

PARMESAN CHILLI SPAGHETTI FRITTERS

Preparation: 10 minutes
Cooking: 10 minutes

62

serves 4

200 g (7 oz) spaghetti, cooked according
   to the packet instructions, cooled
2 eggs, plus 1 extra yolk
small bunch of coriander (cilantro), plus extra to
   garnish, leaves picked and roughly chopped
150 g (5 oz) grated Parmesan-style cheese
1 teaspoon salt
60 ml (2 fl oz/¼ cup) Green Chilli Oil (page 14)

method

Using kitchen scissors, cut the cooked spaghetti roughly into 2–3 cm (1 in) pieces over a bowl. Add all the remaining ingredients except the oil to the bowl and mix well. Heat the chilli oil in a frying pan (skillet) over medium–high heat and fry spoonfuls of mixture until golden on both sides. It should make 8–10. Season with extra salt and garnish with extra coriander.

ASPARAGUS TART

Preparation: 5 minutes
Cooking: 15 minutes

64

serves 4

1 piece focaccia (250 g/9 oz) cut in half horizontally
2 tablespoons extra-virgin olive oil
460 g (1 lb 2 oz) asparagus, trimmed
1 garlic clove, peeled and thinly sliced
small handful of thyme
½ lemon, sliced into thin rounds
160 g (5¾ oz) labneh or vegan sour cream
salt and freshly ground black pepper

method

Preheat the oven to 220°C (425°F/Gas 7). Drizzle the cut sides of the focaccia halves with 1 tablespoon of the olive oil and toast until golden. Remove from the oven and set aside. Meanwhile, toss the asparagus with the remaining olive oil, garlic and several thyme sprigs. Season well and roast with the sliced lemon for 15 minutes, or until tender and slightly charred. Spread the focaccia halves with labneh or sour cream. Arrange the asparagus over the bread, top with the remaining thyme and charred lemon and slice into squares to serve.

PANEER DUMPLINGS

Preparation: 10 minutes
Cooking: 5 minutes

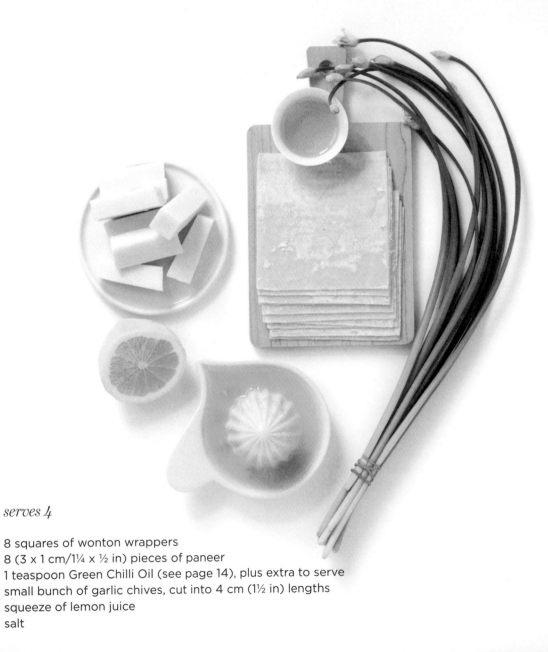

66

serves 4

8 squares of wonton wrappers
8 (3 x 1 cm/1¼ x ½ in) pieces of paneer
1 teaspoon Green Chilli Oil (see page 14), plus extra to serve
small bunch of garlic chives, cut into 4 cm (1½ in) lengths
squeeze of lemon juice
salt

method

Separate each wonton wrapper and place a piece of paneer in the middle of each one. Wet the edges of each wrapper with a little water, then bring 2 edges together and fold to create a triangle. Heat the oil in a frying pan (skillet) over medium–high heat and fry the dumplings for 3 minutes, or until golden on both sides. Add 2 tablespoons water, cover with a lid and steam for 2 minutes until the water has evaporated and the dumplings are cooked. Remove the pan lid and fry for another 30 seconds. Season with salt and serve with extra chilli oil, garlic chives and a squeeze of lemon juice.

SPICY PAPPADUM BRUSCHETTA

Preparation: 15 minutes

serves 4

4 pappadums, fried until puffed and golden,
  then cooled and halved
4 tablespoons Roasted Garlic Dressing (see page 14)
1 quantity of Peach Salsa (see page 20)
pinch of habanero or red chilli powder
salt
1 lime, cut into 8 wedges, to serve

method

Spread each piece of pappadum with ½ tablespoon of the dressing, then spoon over the salsa. Sprinkle with chilli powder and salt to taste. Serve with lime wedges.

HALLOUMI SLIDERS

Preparation: 35 minutes

serves 4

100 g (3½ oz) Spicy Beetroot Relish (see page 26)
100 g (3½ oz) crème fraîche or sour cream
4 mini burger buns, lightly toasted
310 g (11 oz) halloumi, sliced into 8 pieces, fried until golden
    on all sides
½ avocado, peeled, pitted and sliced
small handful of watercress
salt

method

Combine the beetroot relish and crème fraîche in a bowl. Spread over the bottom half of each bun. Top each with 2 slices of halloumi, avocado and some watercress, then sprinkle with a pinch of salt. Put the lid on each burger and serve.

ROAST POTATOES WITH GARLIC DRESSING

Preparation: 10 minutes
Cooking: 40–60 minutes

serves 4

450 g (1 lb) small roasting potatoes, skin on and halved
2 tablespoons extra-virgin olive oil
1 teaspoon sumac
salt and freshly ground black pepper
small bunch of garlic chives, cut into 2 cm (¾ in) batons
1 quantity of Roasted Garlic Dressing (see page 14), to serve

method

Place a rimmed baking tray (sheet) in the oven and preheat the oven to 240°C (475°F/ Gas 8). Combine the potatoes, olive oil and half the sumac in a large bowl. Season with a generous pinch of salt and pepper and toss until well combined. Arrange the potatoes on the heated tray, cut-sides down, and roast for 45–60 minutes until browned and tender. Transfer to a large bowl and garnish with remaining sumac and the chives. Serve with the dressing.

SUNRISE PITTA POCKETS

Preparation: 10 minutes
Cooking: 10 minutes

74

serves 4

4 mini pitta breads, sliced through the top to make an opening
8 eggs, scrambled, seasoned and cooked until silky
1 avocado, peeled, pitted and sliced
150 g (5½ oz) Citrus & Herb Feta (see page 54)
1 tablespoon Celebration Dukkah (see page 50)
large bunch of coriander (cilantro), leaves picked
1 lemon, cut into half slices, to serve

method

Using your hand, gently widen the opening of each pitta bread to create an internal pocket. Fill each pocket with scrambled egg, avocado, feta, dukkah and finish with coriander. Serve with lemon slices.

VEGETABLE BÁHN MI

Preparation: 10 minutes

serves 4

2 tablespoons mayonnaise
1 teaspoon sriracha sauce
500 g (1 lb 2 oz) raw vegetables such as carrots, cucumbers,
   radishes and cabbage, thinly sliced or shredded
2 tablespoons white wine vinegar
1 baguette, split open lengthways
salt
small bunch of mint, to garnish

method

Combine the mayonnaise and sriracha in a small bowl. In another bowl, toss the vegetables with the vinegar and season well with salt. Spread the halved baguette with sriracha mayonnaise and fill with the prepared vegetables, then cut baguette into small pieces and garnish with mint.

SPICY HALLOUMI 'SOUVLAKI'

Preparation: 10 minutes
Cooking: 10 minutes

78

serves 2

310 g (11 oz) halloumi, cut into 16 cubes
4 rosemary sprigs
1 tablespoon extra-virgin olive oil
½ teaspoon red chilli (hot pepper) flakes
salt
4 lemon halves, to serve
4 tablespoons Fennel, Mint & Caraway Tzatziki (see page 44),
    to serve

method

Using a skewer, pierce each halloumi cube, then gently thread 4 pieces onto each rosemary sprig, allowing space between each cube. Heat the olive oil in a frying pan (skillet) over medium heat and fry the skewers for 1–2 minutes on each side or until golden. Sprinkle with chilli flakes and season with salt. Serve with lemon halves and tzatziki.

JUMBO STUFFED PASTA SHELLS

Preparation: 25 minutes
Cooking: 10 minutes

80

serves 4

120 g (4¼ oz) fresh ricotta
60 g (2 oz) finely grated Parmesan-style cheese, plus extra
   for sprinkling
80 g (2¾ oz) Tuscan Marinated Olives (see page 146), pitted and
   roughly chopped, plus 1 tablespoon of the marinating oil
small handful of baby spinach, roughly chopped
16 jumbo pasta shells (450 g/1 lb packet), cooked according to the
   packet instructions, cooled
salt
small handful of basil leaves, roughly torn, to serve

method

Combine both cheeses, the olives, oil and spinach in a bowl and season with salt to taste.
Divide the mixture among the pasta shells and sprinkle over a little extra grated cheese.
Place under a preheated grill (broiler) for about 10 minutes until the cheese is melted and
the edges of the pasta shells are crisp and golden. Scatter over the basil leaves and serve.

SQUASHED GARLIC BUTTER BEAN BITES

Preparation: 10 minutes
Cooking: 10 minutes

82

serves 4

1 Lebanese flatbread, torn into 8 pieces and wrapped in foil

400 g (14 oz) tin butter beans, drained and rinsed

4 tablespoons butter

3 garlic cloves, peeled and finely sliced

1 small red onion, finely diced

salt

1 quantity of Spiced Guacamole (see page 48), lime wedges and
   coriander (cilantro) leaves, to serve

method

Preheat the oven to 150°C (300°F/Gas 3). Warm the wrapped bread in the oven for
10 minutes. Meanwhile, heat the butter in a frying pan (skillet) over medium heat and fry
the garlic for 30 seconds until fragrant. Add the onion and fry until soft. Increase the heat
to high, add the beans and a generous pinch of salt and fry for 2 minutes until the skins are
blistering and golden brown. Cool until warm, then squash with a fork, leaving some beans
whole. Remove the flatbread from the oven and top with the beans. Serve with guacamole,
lime wedges and coriander.

MINI 'SOCIAL DOGS'

Preparation: 15 minutes
Cooking: 6 minutes

serves 4

4 mini brioche or similar hot dog buns,
   cut lengthways without going all the way through
1 tablespoon mild English mustard
150 g (5 oz) grated smoked English 'red' Cheddar
4 round lettuce leaves, torn in half
4 Vegan Chipolatas (see page 136), cooked and kept warm
50 g (1¾ oz) Cucumber Pickle (see page 15), roughly chopped
½ Granny Smith apple, cored and sliced into matchsticks
   with a mandoline

method

Spread each bun with mustard then fill with cheese. Place under a preheated grill (broiler) for about 6 minutes until melted. Fill each bun with lettuce, a chipolata, pickle and apple.

ROSEMARY, ORANGE & GARLIC FOCACCIA

Preparation: 5 minutes
Cooking: 15 minutes

serves 6

1 large plain focaccia
1 rosemary sprig, leaves picked
5 garlic cloves, peeled
½ teaspoon salt
finely grated zest of 1 orange
2 tablespoons extra-virgin olive oil
1 quantity of Beetroot Dip (see page 36), to serve

method

Preheat the oven to 200°C (400°F/Gas 6). Using a small sharp knife, pierce holes all over the top of the focaccia. Crush the rosemary, garlic, salt and orange zest in a mortar and pestle to form a chunky paste, then stir in the oil. Smear over the focaccia, pushing paste into the holes. Wrap in foil and bake in oven for 10 minutes. Open the top of the foil and bake for another 5 minutes, or until golden. Serve in chunks with beetroot dip.

SWEET POTATO FRIES & AVOCADO CREAM

Preparation: 10 minutes
Cooking: 25 minutes

serves 4

2 sweet potatoes, cut into thin batons
4 tablespoons extra-virgin olive oil
salt
2 ripe avocados, peeled, pitted and roughly chopped
juice of 2 limes
4 tablespoons Pesto (see page 32), add more extra-virgin olive oil
   if needed to create a runny consistency, to serve

method

Preheat the oven to 200°C (400°F/Gas 6). Toss the sweet potato batons in 2 tablespoons of the olive oil and a generous pinch of salt on a baking tray. Roast for 25 minutes until soft inside and golden on the outside. Blend the avocados, remaining olive oil, lime juice and a pinch of salt in a food processor until smooth and creamy. Serve with the fries and pesto.

MINI VEGGIE 'GYROS'

Preparation: 30 minutes

serves 4

8 tablespoons Roasted Garlic Dressing (see page 14)
2 pitta breads, quartered (8 pieces in total)
4 baby gem (bibb) lettuce leaves, halved
2 portobello mushrooms, stems removed,
  thickly sliced and fried until golden
4 Vegan Chipolatas (see page 136), halved
¼ small red onion, finely sliced
½ teaspoon dried oregano

method

Spread ½ tablespoon of the garlic dressing over each piece of flatbread using the back of a spoon. Divide the lettuce and mushrooms between the pittas, then top with half a chipolata and a few slices of onion. Drizzle over the remaining garlic dressing and sprinkle with oregano. Roll up the bread leaving both ends open and secure with a toothpick.

BAKED BLACK SESAME CAMEMBERT

Preparation: 5 minutes
Cooking: 20 minutes

serves 4

250 g (9 oz) wheel of Camembert
5 thyme sprigs
2 tablespoons honey
½ teaspoon black sesame seeds
50 g (2 oz) flaked (sliced) almonds, lightly toasted
1 long red chilli, thinly sliced on a diagonal
1 small baguette, thickly sliced, to serve

method

Preheat the oven to 180°C (350°F/Gas 4). Score the top of cheese around the edge, about 5 mm (¼ in) in, and cut off the top layer of skin. Poke thyme into the top of the cheese, then bake for 20 minutes, or until oozy in the middle. Drizzle over the honey, then sprinkle over the remaining ingredients. Serve with baguette.

BASIL & GOAT'S CHEESE FRITTATA

Preparation: 15 minutes
Cooking: 10 minutes

94

serves 4

6 eggs
small bunch of basil, leaves picked and
   finely shredded, plus extra to garnish,
4 tablespoons butter
40 g (1½ oz) goat's cheese
salt and freshly ground black pepper
4 tablespoons Spicy Beetroot Relish (see page 26), to serve

BRAINSE CARNAN CLOCH
DOLPHINS BARN LIBRARY
TEL. 454 0681

method

Whisk the eggs, basil and a pinch of salt and pepper together. Melt the butter in an ovenproof frying pan (skillet), then pour in the egg mixture. Cook for 2 minutes, then carefully take the pan off the heat. Crumble the cheese over the frittata and place under a preheated grill (broiler) for 7 minutes, or until set and golden on top. Once cool enough to handle, remove the frittata from the pan and cut it into 8 pieces. Scatter over some more basil and serve warm or cold with beetroot relish.

SPANIKOPITA CIGARS

Preparation: 20 minutes
Cooking: 30 minutes

makes 9

140 g (5 oz) baby spinach, sautéed and excess liquid squeezed
    out or frozen spinach, thawed and excess liquid squeezed
1 small leek, finely diced and sautéed
200 g (7 oz) ricotta
small bunch of dill, leaves picked and finely chopped
½ teaspoon salt
6 large square sheets of frozen filo pastry, thawed
60 ml (2 fl oz/¼ cup) extra-virgin olive oil

method

Mix the spinach, leek, ricotta, dill and salt together. Chill. Preheat the oven to 180°C (350°F/Gas 4). Take a filo sheet and brush it with oil. Top with a second sheet and brush again. Repeat, then cut across the filo square twice in each direction to make 9 smaller squares. Take a square and place a heaped tablespoon of filling in the centre of the bottom edge. Roll the filling up a little, then tuck in the sides. Brush with oil, then finish rolling up tightly. Repeat. Place the cigars seam-side down on a baking-paper-lined tray. Bake until crisp.

CRISPY DELICATA SQUASH RINGS

Preparation: 30 minutes
Cooking: 15 minutes

98

serves 4

½ teaspoon salt, plus extra for sprinkling
2 Delicata squash or small butternut squash,
   sliced into 1.5 cm (½ in) rings and deseeded
3 tablespoons extra-virgin olive oil
juice and zest of 1 lime
1 tablespoon Celebration Dukkah (see page 50)

method

Lightly salt the squash and leave for 30 minutes. Dry with kitchen paper, removing the salt. Heat the oil in a large pan over medium-high heat. Season the squash rings with the ½ teaspoon salt and add to the pan. Sauté in batches until golden brown, about 2 minutes on each side. Remove and squeeze over the lime juice. Scatter over the lime zest and dukkah.

CHUTNEY EGGS

Preparation: 5 minutes
Cooking: 7 minutes

serves 4

4 eggs
100 g (3½ oz) Tomato Chutney (see page 28)
2 tablespoons sour cream
few thyme sprigs
salt and freshly ground black pepper

method

Boil the eggs for 7 minutes, or to the desired doneness. Peel and halve each egg, shaving a tiny amount off the bottom of each so the halves sit upright. Top with chutney and sour cream and garnish with thyme. Season to taste.

FENNEL SEED CRACKERS

Preparation: 15 minutes
Cooking: 10 minutes

serves 4

240 g (8½ oz/ 1¾ cups) spelt flour
1 teaspoon salt, plus extra for sprinkling
125 ml (4⅓ fl oz/½ cup) extra-virgin olive oil
2 teaspoons fennel seeds
200 g (7 oz) block of feta
1 quantity of Beetroot Dip (see page 36)

method

Preheat the oven to 180°C (350°F/Gas 4). Mix the flour, salt, oil and fennel seeds together with 180 ml (6 fl oz/¾ cup) water, then divide the mixture into handful-sized balls. Roll each out as thinly as you can and place on baking-paper-lined baking trays. Bake for 10 minutes, or until golden and crisp. Cool slightly and break up. Sprinkle with extra salt, and serve with feta and the beetroot dip.

RADISHES WITH MISO BUTTER

Preparation: 5 minutes

104

serves 4

1 tablespoon white miso paste
1 tablespoon soft butter
1 tablespoon lemon juice
small bunch of baby radishes, stalks trimmed to 4 cm (1½ in),
  radishes halved

method

Mix the miso, butter and lemon juice together in a bowl until combined. Place the radishes on a serving plate and dollop miso butter on top of each radish.

THAI CUCUMBER OPEN SANDWICHES

Preparation: 15 minutes

serves 2

1 tablespoon Green Chilli Oil (see page 14)
2 teaspoons rice vinegar
½ teaspoon salt, plus extra for sprinkling
1 small cucumber (about 85 g/3 oz), thinly sliced on a mandoline
2 slices of soft white sandwich bread, halved, crusts removed
30 g (1 oz) raw peanuts, roasted and roughly chopped
2 eggs, soft-boiled in boiling water for 5 minutes,
   cooled, then peeled

method

Whisk the oil, vinegar and salt together in a bowl. Add the cucumber slices and coat well in the dressing. Lay the 4 pieces of bread out, arrange cucumber slices in rows on each piece, then sprinkle over the peanuts. Carefully halve each egg and arrange on each sandwich. Sprinkle an extra pinch of salt over each sandwich and serve.

CRUDITÉS WITH GARLIC DRESSING

Preparation: 15 minutes
Cooking: 30 minutes

serves 4

145 g (5¼ oz) baby beetroot
   (beets)
3 eggs
275 g (9¾ oz) asparagus, trimmed
85 g (3 oz) sugar snap peas, trimmed
140 g (5 oz) radishes, sliced
80 g (2¾ oz) cherry tomatoes, halved
salt and freshly ground black pepper
1 quantity of Roasted Garlic Dressing (see page 14)

method

Boil the beetroot until tender and soft boil the eggs. Blanch the asparagus and sugar snap peas in a pan of salted water until bright green but still crisp. Arrange the prepared asparagus, sugar snap peas, radishes and tomatoes on a serving platter. Peel and halve the beetroot and eggs. Season well. Serve with the garlic dressing

'CAESAR SALAD' BITES

Preparation: 10 minutes
Cooking: 10 minutes

serves 4

4 slices of sourdough (5 mm/¼ in thick), baked at
   200°C (400°F/Gas 6) until crisp, then broken in half
4 tablespoons Roasted Garlic Dressing (see page 14)
1 baby gem leaf, torn into 8 pieces
90 g (3¼ oz) halloumi, sliced into 8 pieces and fried until golden
salt
20 g (¾ oz) grated Parmesan-style cheese
½ lemon, cut into wedges, to serve

method

Spread the 8 sourdough pieces with a layer of dressing, reserving some. Put a piece of lettuce and halloumi on top, then dollop on the reserved dressing. Top with grated cheese and season with salt. Repeat to prepare 8 bites, then serve with lemon wedges.

PARMESAN CRISPS WITH TABASCO

Preparation: 5 minutes
Cooking: 5 minutes

serves 4

100 g (1½ cups) finely grated Parmesan-style cheese
2 tablespoons flaxseeds
2 teaspoons fennel seeds, lightly toasted
6 thyme sprigs, leaves picked and roughly chopped
salt
bottle of Tabasco sauce, to serve

method

Preheat the oven to 250°C (480°F/Gas 9). Line a baking tray (sheet) with baking paper. Combine the cheese, flaxseeds, fennel seeds and thyme leaves in a bowl. Spread over the baking paper in a single, even layer and bake for 5 minutes, or until golden and crisp. Cool, then break into pieces. Season with salt and serve with Tabasco sauce.

HASSELBACK BABY BEETROOT WITH FETA

Preparation: 10 minutes
Cooking: 50–60 minutes

114

serves 4

8 mixed golden and red baby
   beetroot (beets), scrubbed, stalks trimmed
60 ml (2 fl oz/¼ cup) extra-virgin olive oil
10 thyme sprigs, leaves picked
1 teaspoon salt
150 g (5½ oz) Citrus & Herb Feta (see page 54)
40 g (1½ oz) hazelnuts, roasted, skinned and roughly chopped
1 tablespoon orange blossom water

method

Preheat the oven to 200°C (400°F/Gas 6). Cut a small slice from each beetroot lengthways to create a flat side. Place each beetroot, cut-side down, on a baking-paper-lined baking tray (sheet) and deeply score at 5 mm (¼ in) intervals. (Be careful not to cut all the way through.) Combine the olive oil, thyme and salt and brush over the beetroot and into the grooves. Roast for 50–60 minutes until tender and the edges are slightly crisp. Crumble over the feta for the final 10 minutes of cooking to soften. Sprinkle over the hazelnuts and drizzle with orange blossom water.

FETA WITH SUGAR SNAP PEAS

Preparation: 5 minutes
Cooking: 5 minutes

serves 4

230 g (8 oz) feta, cut into 2 cm (¾ in) cubes
2 tablespoons extra-virgin olive oil
2 tablespoons fennel seeds
small handful of pea tendrils
85 g (3 oz) sugar snap peas, blanched
small handful of chives with flowers, if possible

method

Brush the top of each feta cube with a little olive oil, then press fennel seeds into the feta so that they stick. Top each feta cube with a pea tendril. Heat the remaining oil in a non-stick frying pan (skillet) over medium heat. Fry the cheese, seasoned-side down, for 4 minutes, or until golden and just starting to melt. Arrange on a platter and serve with sugar snap peas and chives.

JEWELLED PILAF CUPS WITH TZATZIKI

Preparation: 40 minutes

118

serves 4

90 g (3¼ oz) brown rice, rinsed, cooked and
    cooled completely
½ teaspoon salt
seeds from 1 pomegranate
2½ tablespoons extra-virgin olive oil, plus extra for baby gem
    (bibb) leaves
30 g (1 oz) almonds, roasted and roughly chopped
8 baby gem (bibb) leaves
4 tablespoons Fennel, Mint & Caraway Tzatziki (see page 44)
mint sprigs, to garnish

method

Mix the cooked rice, salt, pomegranate seeds, olive oil and almonds together in a bowl. Rub a little extra olive oil over the lettuce leaves and divide the rice mixture among them. Top each filled leaf with the tzatziki and serve garnished with mint.

MIDDLE EASTERN BITES

Preparation: 20 minutes

serves 4

150 g (5½ oz) labneh
1 large flatbread, roughly torn into 8 pieces
1 teaspoon ras el hanout spice blend, dry-roasted
4 Vegan Chipolatas (see page 136), cooked, each torn into 4 pieces
½ small red onion, finely diced
1 tablespoon pomegranate molasses
handful of mint leaves, finely chopped

method

Spread the labneh over the flatbread 'bites'. Sprinkle over the ras el hanout, then add 2 pieces of chipolata to each. Scatter over the onion, drizzle with molasses, then sprinkle over the mint.

AUBERGINE SANDWICHES

Preparation: 35 minutes

serves 6

2 very small aubergines (eggplants), cut into 12 x 2 cm (¾ in)
   thick slices, roasted until golden on both sides
2½ tablespoons Roasted Garlic Dressing (see page 14)
6 thick slices of goat's cheese
2½ tablespoons Pesto (see page 32), plus extra to serve
small handful of rocket (arugula), plus extra to serve
juice of 1 lime

method

To assemble, place a slice of aubergine on a work surface and spread over 1 teaspoon of the garlic dressing. Top with a slice of cheese, 1 teaspoon of pesto and a few rocket leaves, then squeeze over a little lime juice. Sandwich with another slice of aubergine. Repeat with the remaining ingredients and serve with extra pesto and rocket on top.

ASPARAGUS DIPPERS

Preparation: 20 minutes
Cooking: 10 minutes

124

serves 2

1 egg white, lightly whisked
3 tablespoons Celebration Dukka (see page 50)
9 asparagus, trimmed
salt
1 quantity of Cauliflower Dip with Wasabi Peas (see page 38),
    to serve

method

Preheat the oven to 220°C (425°F/Gas 7). Place the egg white and dukkah onto 2 separate wide, flat plates. Roll each asparagus spear into the egg white, then through the plate of dukkah, completely covering the spears. Sprinkle over a pinch of salt. Roast the dukkah-crusted spears on a baking-paper-lined baking tray (sheet) for 10 minutes until the fattest spear can be pierced with a knife easily and the spears are golden brown. Cool slightly. Serve with the cauliflower dip with wasabi peas.

GRILLED CUCUMBERS WITH WHIPPED FETA

Preparation: 15 minutes
Cooking: 10 minutes

126

serves 4

250 g (9 oz) Citrus & Herb Feta (see page 54),
  drained and finely crumbled
85 g (3 oz) cream cheese
small bunch of dill, leaves picked and roughly chopped
10 mini gherkin cucumbers, halved lengthways
2 tablespoons extra-virgin olive oil
salt
1 lemon, halved and grilled for 2–3 minutes, or until charred, to serve

method

Combine the feta, cream cheese and dill in a food processor and pulse for 4–5 minutes, scraping down the sides of the bowl occasionally, until the feta is smooth and super creamy. Transfer to a bowl. Lightly brush the cucumbers with oil and season with a pinch of salt. Working in batches if necessary, cook the cucumbers under a preheated grill (broiler) for 1–2 minutes on each side until slightly softened and browned. Serve with the whipped feta and charred lemons on the side.

OVEN-ROASTED LATKES

Preparation: 5 minutes
Cooking: 60 minutes

serves 4

12 small potatoes, such as Yukon Gold
extra-virgin olive oil, for drizzling
70 g (2½ oz) sour cream
½ small red onion, thinly sliced
2 tablespoons drained capers
salt and freshly ground black pepper
small handful of chives, snipped, to garnish

method

Preheat the oven to 220°C (425°F/Gas 7). Boil the potatoes until tender. Drain and cool slightly. Use the palm of your hand to flatten to a roughly 5 mm (¼ in) thick, ragged disc. Arrange the potatoes on a well-oiled baking tray. Drizzle with a little more oil and season. Roast for 30 minutes, or until crisp and golden. Remove from the oven and top with sour cream, onions and capers. Garnish with snipped chives.

PEACH SALSA WITH CHEESE CROSTINI

Preparation: 25 minutes

130

serves 4

8 small slices of baguette
2 tablespoons extra-virgin olive oil
150 g (5½ oz) goat's cheese, at room temperature
1 tablespoon milk
1 quantity of Peach Salsa (see page 20)
salt and freshly ground black pepper

method

Preheat the oven to 190°C (375°F/Gas 5). Arrange the baguette slices on a baking tray, (sheet) drizzle over the olive oil and bake on the upper rack for about 4 minutes. Remove, turn over and bake for another 4 minutes. Cool completely. Put the goat's cheese in a small bowl, add the milk and mix well. Spread one side of the baguette with ½ tablespoon of the chèvre, place a heaped spoonful of salsa on top and season to taste.

AVOCADO NAAN

Preparation: 10 minutes

serves 6

1 piece of naan bread
2 avocados
salt
juice of 1 lemon
80 ml (2¾ fl oz/⅓ cup) light tahini
seeds from ½ pomegranate
35 g (1¼ oz) coconut flakes, toasted
large handful of coriander (cilantro) leaves, roughly chopped
extra-virgin olive oil, to drizzle (optional)

method

Toast the naan until golden. Peel and pit the avocados and mash to a loose chunky purée.
Season with salt and half the lemon juice. Whisk together the tahini and the remaining
lemon juice, then whisk in 100 ml (3½ fl oz/scant ½ cup) iced water until smooth. Season
with salt. Spread the naan with the tahini sauce and top with the pomegranate seeds,
coconut and coriander. Drizzle with olive oil, if liked.

VEGAN
made simple

Impress your guests with an eclectic variety of stylish,
plant-based finger food influenced by American, Afghani, Mexican
and Japanese cuisines. Make a few plates to pass around or fill
the table with a selection for a substantial spread.

VEGAN CHIPOLATAS

Preparation: 15 minutes
Cooking: 20 minutes

136

makes 10–14 chipolatas

450 g (1 lb) cooked chickpeas (garbanzo beans)
250 g (9 oz) Portobello and white button mushrooms, fried until golden
4 spring onions (scallions), including green part, chopped and fried until soft
60 g (2 oz) almond flour
4 tablespoons potato starch
3 tablespoons vegan Worcestershire sauce
1 teaspoon achiote powder or pinch of smoked chilli powder,
   mixed with 2 teaspoons water to make a runny paste

method

Preheat oven to 180°C (350°F/Gas 4). Combine all the ingredients in a food processor and pulse until well combined but not completely smooth. With wet hands, roll into small sausages using roughly 1½ tablespoons mixture per chipolata. Bake for 20 minutes, or until golden, but moist inside.

MARINATED TEMPEH

Preparation: 10 minutes

138

makes 600 g (1 lb 5 oz)

2 long red chillies, deseeded
6 garlic cloves, peeled
15 g (½ oz) piece of ginger, peeled and roughly chopped
1 bunch of coriander (cilantro)
1 lemongrass stalk
600 g (1 lb 5 oz) tempeh, cut into 4 cm (1½ in) cubes
500 ml (17 fl oz/2 cups) extra-virgin olive oil

method

Place all the ingredients except the tempeh and oil into a food processor and whizz until roughly chopped. Combine the marinade with the tempeh and transfer to a large sterilised jar. Pour in the olive oil to cover, press down the tempeh to ensure it stays below the oil and seal with lid. Refrigerate for up to a week.

MINI VEG TACOS WITH CHIPOTLE MAYO

Preparation: 30 minutes

serves 2

100 g (3½ oz) Vegan Mayo (see page 15)

2 teaspoons chipotle in adobo, crushed into a paste

4 tablespoons Spiced Guacamole (see page 48)

10–12 salted, round corn chips

1 lime, cut into wedges, to serve (optional)

100 g (3½ oz) broccoli, broken into finger-sized florets, seasoned,
    roasted at 200°C (400°F/Gas 6) until edges are crispy

100 g (3½ oz) cauliflower, broken into finger-sized florets, seasoned,
    roasted at 200°C (400°F/Gas 6) until golden and edges are crispy

method

Stir the chipotle paste into the mayo until well combined. To assemble the tacos, dollop the guacamole onto the corn chips, then place a piece each of cauliflower and broccoli on top and drizzle over a little chipotle mayo. Repeat with all the remaining ingredients. Serve with lime wedges, if liked.

AFGHAN PIZZA

Preparation: 10 minutes
Cooking: 10–15 minutes

142

serves 4

1 Afghan bread (about 350 g/12 oz) or thick flatbread,
   halved horizontally
100 g (3½ oz) Cashew Ricotta (see page 18)
150 g (5 oz) cherry tomatoes, sliced
2 tablespoons olive oil, plus extra to drizzle
salt
1 tablespoon Celebration Dukkah (see page 50)
handful of mint leaves

method

Preheat the oven to 200°C (400°F/Gas 6). Spread the cut sides of the bread with ricotta and top with the tomatoes and olive oil. Season with salt. Bake for 10–15 minutes until the edges are golden. Drizzle over extra olive oil and sprinkle with dukkah and mint.

AUBERGINE KARAAGE WITH TEMPEH

Preparation: 15 minutes + Marination: 15 minutes
Cooking: 10 minutes

serves 4

60 ml (2 fl oz/¼ cup) tamari
2 tablespoons mirin
25 g (1 oz) piece of ginger, finely grated and squeezed to reserve
   juice, discard flesh
1 large aubergine (eggplant), sliced into 1 cm (½ in) thick rounds
150 g (5 oz) potato flour
500 ml (17 fl oz/2 cups) rice bran oil or vegetable oil
80 g (2¾ oz) Marinated Tempeh (see page 138), to serve

method

Combine the tamari, mirin and ginger juice in a bowl, then pour it over the aubergine, turning to coat. Marinate for 15 minutes. Place the flour in a bowl and drop the marinated aubergine into the flour, a piece at a time, turning to coat, then remove. Repeat until all the aubergine is coated. Heat the oil in a large wok or saucepan to 190°C (375°F). Shake off any excess flour from the aubergine, then deep-fry for 2–3 minutes until golden on both sides. Transfer to a wire rack to rest for 30 seconds. Serve with the tempeh.

TUSCAN MARINATED OLIVES

Preparation: 10 minutes
Marination: 7 days

serves 4

1½ tablespoons coriander seeds
1 teaspoon fennel seeds
6 garlic cloves, peeled and crushed
1 rosemary sprig
200 ml (7 fl oz/scant 1 cup) extra-virgin olive oil
400 g (14 oz) mixed olives, such as green, Kalamata and black
zest of 1 orange, cut or peeled into thick strips

method

Lightly crush the coriander and fennel seeds in a mortar and pestle, keeping some whole. Place the garlic, rosemary and oil in a small pan and heat until just warm. Layer the olives, orange zest and spices in a sterilised jar, then pour over the warm oil including the garlic and rosemary. Seal. Turn the jar upside down and stand for 5 minutes. Turn upright. Leave for a week in refrigerator, turning once daily. Remove from the refrigerator 1 hour before serving.

CRISPY TOFU WITH ORANGE & MACADAMIA

Preparation: 15 minutes

serves 4

1 blood orange or Valencia orange, peeled, segmented and diced

80 g (2¾ oz) firm tofu, diced, seasoned and fried until golden
and crispy

3 tablespoons macadamia nuts, ½ chopped, ½ left whole

small handful of coriander (cilantro) leaves, chopped,
plus extra whole leaves to garnish

60 ml (2 fl oz/¼ cup) extra-virgin olive oil, plus extra for the endive

2 tablespoons raspberry wine vinegar or balsamic vinegar

8 small purple endive or chicory leaves

method

Combine the orange, tofu, chopped macadamias and chopped coriander in a bowl. Whisk the oil and vinegar together in another bowl and pour the mixture over the tofu. Rub a little oil over the endive and spoon the dressed mixture on top of the leaves. Finely grate whole macadamias over the top and garnish with coriander.

CAULIFLOWER BHAJIS

Preparation: 30 minutes
Cooking: 10 minutes

150

serves 6

130 g (4½ oz) chickpea (gram) flour
1 teaspoon salt, plus extra to season
½ teaspoon baking powder
2 teaspoons cumin seeds
700 ml (1 lb 9 oz) sunflower oil
½ head of cauliflower, (about 500 g/1 lb 2 oz) broken into florets,
    soaked in water with 1 teaspoon salt for 30 minutes,
    then drained and patted dry
salt
1 quantity of Tomato Chutney (see page 28), to serve

method

Make a batter by whisking together the flour, salt, baking powder, cumin seeds and 125 ml (4⅓ fl oz/½ cup) water in a bowl. Heat the oil in a small saucepan or wok over high heat. Test the temperature by dropping a little batter into the oil – it should quickly spring up to the surface. Dip all the cauliflower pieces into the batter and fry in batches until golden brown. Season generously with salt, then serve with the chutney on side.

CHARGRILLED MEXICAN CORN

Preparation: 5 minutes
Cooking: 10 minutes

152

serves 2

1 tablespoon vegetable oil
1 corn-on-the-cob/ear of corn, husk removed
1 teaspoon white miso paste
2 tablespoons Vegan Mayo (see page 15)
¼ teaspoon fennel seeds, lightly toasted
pinch of chilli powder
salt

method

Heat a frying pan and brush with oil. When the pan begins to smoke, add the corn and chargrill on all sides for about 6 minutes. Once cool enough to handle, slice the corn into 8 rounds. Meanwhile, combine the miso and mayo. Dollop the miso mixture on top of the corn, then sprinkle over the fennel seeds and chilli powder. Season with salt to taste.

CRUNCHY MEXICAN CHICKPEA BOWL

Preparation: 5 minutes
Cooking: 30 minutes

154

serves 2

400 g (14 oz) tin chickpeas (garbanzo beans), drained and rinsed
1 tablespoon extra-virgin olive oil
½ teaspoon salt
1 teaspoon dried coriander leaves
1 teaspoon ground cumin
½ teaspoon garlic powder
¼ teaspoon hot paprika

method

Preheat the oven to 200°C (400°F/Gas 6). Gently roll the chickpeas between two tea towels to make them as dry as possible. Toss the chickpeas in olive oil and salt, then spread onto a baking-paper-lined tray in a single layer. Roast for 20 minutes, or until golden and crispy. stirring halfway through cooking. Turn the oven off, keep the door ajar slightly and leave the chickpeas inside for a little longer to crisp up. Remove from the oven, toss in the dried herb and spices, and serve hot.

PARSNIP CHIPS WITH PESTO

Preparation: 15 minutes
Cooking: 25 minutes

serves 4

500 g (1 lb 2 oz) parsnips, scrubbed and sliced into thin rounds
2 tablespoons extra-virgin olive oil
1 teaspoon salt
½ teaspoon paprika
small bunch of basil leaves, to garnish
small handful of pine nuts, toasted, to garnish
1 quantity of Pesto (see page 32), to serve

method

Preheat the oven to 190°C (375°F/Gas 5). Toss the parsnip rounds with the olive oil, salt and paprika. Bake on a baking-paper-lined tray (sheet) for 25 minutes, or until golden brown, flipping halfway. Remove from the oven, garnish with basil and pine nuts and serve with pesto.

MAPLE PUMPKIN BITES WITH DUKKAH

Preparation: 10 minutes
Cooking: 40 minutes

serves 4

450 g (1 lb) butternut squash
1 tablespoon melted coconut oil
1 tablespoon maple syrup
¼ teaspoon salt
50 g (1¾ oz) Cashew Ricotta (see page 18)
1 tablespoon Celebration Dukkah (see page 50)
handful of coriander (cilantro) leaves, roughly chopped

method

Preheat the oven to 220°C (425°F/Gas 7). Cut the squash into bite-sized chunks, leaving the skin on and seeds intact. Place, skin-side down, on a baking tray (sheet). Drizzle with oil, maple syrup and salt and toss to coat, then roast for 40 minutes, or until soft and the edges are slightly burnt. Cool slightly. Top with a spoonful of ricotta and sprinkle with dukkah and coriander.

TRAIL MIX BITES

Preparation: 10 minutes

160

serves 4

2 Granny Smith apples, peeled if wished
60 g (2 oz) pecan or almond nut butter
6 dried apricots, finely chopped
3 tablespoons pumpkin seeds, chopped
2 tablespoons sunflower seeds, chopped

method

Cut the apples into 1 cm (½ in) thick rounds and remove the seeds. Top each round with a spoonful of nut butter, then pile the apricots, pumpkin seeds and sunflower seeds on top of the butter.

TOMATO CHUTNEY WITH LENTILS

Preparation: 10 minutes

162

serves 4

100 g (10½ oz) cooked green lentils
1 quantity of Tomato Chutney (see page 28)
handful of mini pappadums, fried until crisp
3 tablespoons coconut yoghurt
¼ small cucumber, diced
small handful of mint sprigs

method

Combine the lentils and chutney in a bowl, then spoon the mixture over the fried pappadums. Top with a small dollop of coconut yoghurt, then scatter with diced cucumber and top with mint sprigs.

ARTICHOKE TAPENADE

Preparation: 5 minutes

serves 4

150 g (5 oz) Marinated Artichoke Hearts (see page 176)
Fennel Seed Crackers (see page 102), to serve
65 g (2¼ oz) Romesco Sauce (see page 34)
2 tablespoons pistachio nuts, roughly chopped
salt

method

Remove the artichokes from the marinade and set aside a few thick strips of the citrus zest. Use a food processor to pulse the artichokes and 2 tablespoons of oil from the artichoke jar to a chunky purée. Spoon the purée onto the crackers, along with a dollop of the romesco sauce. Thinly slice the zest. Top the purée with chopped nuts and sliced zest and season with salt.

TEMPEH LARB GAI

Preparation: 10 minutes
Cooking: 6 minutes

166

serves 6

400 g (14 oz) Marinated Tempeh (see page 138), coarsely grated,
  plus 3 tablespoons of the marinating oil with chunks of chilli
  and herbs included
1 small red onion, finely sliced
1 teaspoon coconut palm sugar, finely grated
finely grated zest of 1 lime, plus a squeeze of the juice
small bunch of mint, leaves picked, plus extra to garnish
½ teaspoon salt
4 iceberg lettuce leaves, roughly torn into medium pieces

method

Heat the marinating oil in a frying pan (skillet) over medium-high heat and fry the tempeh for 6 minutes, or until golden and crispy. Take the pan off the heat and stir through the onion, sugar, lime zest and juice, mint and salt. Cool for a minute, then divide between the lettuce pieces. Garnish with extra mint.

RICE PAPER ROLLS

Preparation: 15 minutes
Cooking: 3 minutes

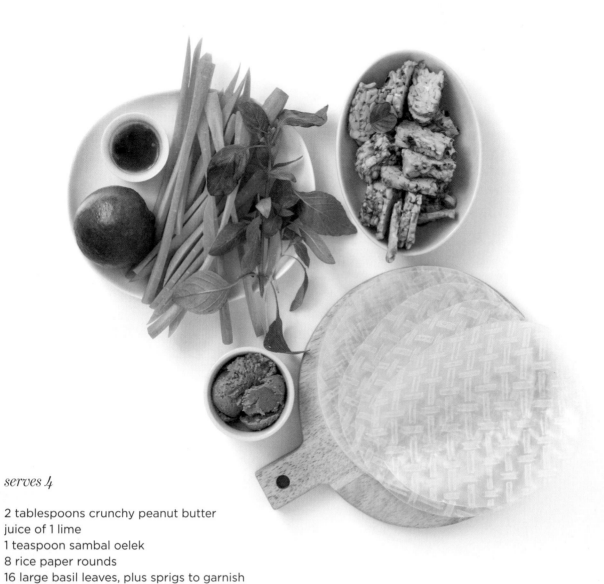

serves 4

2 tablespoons crunchy peanut butter
juice of 1 lime
1 teaspoon sambal oelek
8 rice paper rounds
16 large basil leaves, plus sprigs to garnish
1 small carrot, thinly sliced into batons
200 g (7 oz) Marinated Tempeh (see page 138),
    sliced and fried until golden

method

For the peanut sauce, combine the peanut butter, lime juice and sambal oelek with 2 tablespoons water and mix well. Submerge a rice paper round in a bowl of warm water until just soft, about 15 seconds. Lay flat on a work surface and place 2 basil leaves in the centre, one above the other, then add a few carrot and tempeh slices. Fold the bottom end in and roll up firmly to enclose the filling, leaving contents sticking out of the top. If the sauce has thickened, add a little more water as needed and serve with the rolls, garnished with basil sprigs.

SUSHI RICE ROLLS

Preparation: 5 minutes
Cooking: 40 minutes

Serves 4

400 g (14 oz) sushi rice
1 tablespoon sushi rice vinegar
35 g (1¼ oz) sesame seeds, toasted
matcha (green tea) powder, to taste
2 tablespoons pickled ginger, thinly sliced
6 umeboshi (pickled plums), thinly sliced
salt

method

Cook the sushi rice according to the packet instructions and season with the vinegar.
Using wet hands, shape the rice into balls, each about the size of a small egg. Roll the balls
in sesame seeds, season with matcha or top with ginger and umeboshi plum as desired.
Sprinkle with salt before serving.

CAPRESE STACKS

Preparation: 10 minutes

172

serves 4

1 teaspoon white miso
juice and grated zest of 1 lemon
3 tablespoons black sesame seeds
1 quantity of Cashew Ricotta (see page 18), divided into 16 pieces
  and rolled into balls
4–5 large beefsteak tomatoes, ends removed,
  thickly sliced (need 16 thick slices), seasoned with salt
16 basil leaves, plus sprigs to garnish
salt

method

Whisk the miso and lemon juice and zest together and set aside. Put the sesame seeds in a bowl and roll each ricotta ball through the seeds to coat. To create the stacks, begin with a slice of tomato as a base, then gently press a ball of ricotta on top, followed by a basil leaf. Repeat to create a second layer. Repeat with the remaining ingredients to make 8 stacks. Season with salt to taste, garnish with extra basil and serve with the miso dressing.

PIRI PIRI CAULIFLOWER WITH LIME MAYO

Preparation: 5 minutes
Cooking: 20 minutes

174

serves 4

1 medium cauliflower, broken into florets
1 teaspoon salt
4 tablespoons vegetable oil
2 teaspoons piri piri spice blend
handful of coriander (cilantro) leaves
250 g (9 oz) Vegan Mayo (see page 15)
finely grated zest of 1 lime, plus 1 teaspoon lime juice

method

Preheat the oven to 180°C (350°F/Gas 4). Toss the cauliflower florets with the salt, oil and piri piri and place on a baking tray (sheet). Roast for 20 minutes, or until golden and soft inside. Cool slightly, then sprinkle over the coriander. Mix the mayo with the lime zest and juice and serve on side.

MARINATED ARTICHOKE HEARTS

Preparation: 10 minutes

serves 4

1 bay leaf
juice of 1 lemon, plus the zest pared into thick strips
zest of 1 orange, peeled or cut into thick strips
330 g (11½ oz) whole artichoke hearts
6 whole black peppercorns
1 teaspoon fennel seeds, lightly toasted
250 ml (8¾ fl oz/1 cup) extra-virgin olive oil

method

Place the bay leaf and lemon and orange zest on the inside of a sterilised jar then layer in the artichoke hearts, peppercorns and fennel seeds. Cover with olive oil and squeeze over the lemon juice. Press the contents down to ensure the artichokes are submerged. Seal with the lid and refrigerate for up to 6 months.

PORTOBELLO PIZZAS

Preparation: 20 minutes
Cooking: 30 minutes

178

serves 4

8 small Portobello mushrooms, stalks removed
4 tablespoons extra-virgin olive oil
4 garlic cloves, peeled and crushed
½ teaspoon salt
8 tablespoons Tomato Chutney (see page 28)
50 g (1¾ oz) Cashew Ricotta (see page 18), frozen for 20 minutes
small handful of basil leaves, to garnish

method

Preheat the oven to 200°C (400°F/Gas 6). Place the mushrooms in a baking paper-lined dish (pan). Whisk the oil, garlic and salt together in a bowl and pour over the mushrooms, using your hands to rub it into the flesh. Bake for 20 minutes, then remove and divide the chutney between the mushrooms. Grate over the ricotta and return to the oven for another 10 minutes, or until golden. Season with salt to taste and serve garnished with basil.

MANGO SPEARS WITH LIME & CHILLI

Preparation: 5 minutes

180

serves 4

3 ripe mangoes, peeled, pitted and sliced into thick spears
juice of 1 lime, plus lime halves to serve
salt, to taste
chilli powder, to taste

method

Brush the mango spears with lime juice, then sprinkle them with chilli powder and salt.
Serve with lime halves.

ASIAN AUBERGINE CAPONATA

Preparation: 10 minutes
Cooking: 40 minutes

182

serves 4

1 tablespoon extra-virgin olive oil
1 red onion, diced
1 medium aubergine (eggplant), cut into 1 cm (½ in)
   thick long batons
5 cm (2 in) piece of ginger, peeled and grated
grated zest and juice of 2 limes
large bunch of coriander (cilantro), roughly chopped, plus
   a few sprigs to garnish
1 tablespoon tamari
salt and freshly ground black pepper
crackers, to serve

method

Heat the olive oil in a frying pan (skillet) and cook the onion for 10 minutes, or until soft and translucent. Add the aubergine and ginger and cook, covered, over low heat until the aubergine is very soft, about 30 minutes. Add a splash of water about every 5 minutes to prevent the pan from scorching. Remove the pan from the heat and stir in the lime juice and zest, chopped coriander and tamari, then season. Spoon the mixture over crackers and top with coriander.

WATERMELON 'PIZZA'

Preparation: 10 minutes

184

serves 4

1 small watermelon,
   cut into 2 cm (¾ in) thick rounds
1½ tablespoons extra-virgin olive oil
2 small cucumbers, thinly sliced
handful of edible flowers, such as broccoli
small handful of mint sprigs, leaves picked
seasoned salt of choice

method

Brush the top of each watermelon round with olive oil. Scatter cucumber slices, flowers and mint leaves on top. Season with salt to taste and cut into wedges.

SWEET POTATO 'CROSTINI'

Preparation: 10 minutes
Cooking: 30 minutes

186

serves 4

1 sweet potato, unpeeled, sliced into
    1½ cm (½ in) rounds
1 tablespoon extra-virgin olive oil, plus extra for greasing
195 g (6¾ oz) cooked Puy lentils (110 g/3¾ oz)
2 avocados, peeled, pitted and roughly chopped
50 g (1¾ oz) pumpkin seeds, dry-roasted and salted
small handful of flat-leaf parsley, leaves picked and roughly chopped
salt

method

Preheat the oven to 200°C (400°F/Gas 6). Place the sweet potato rounds in a single layer on a lightly oiled baking tray (sheet) and season with a generous pinch of salt. Roast for 30 minutes until browned on the bottom. Cool slightly. Meanwhile, combine the remaining ingredients in a bowl and mix well. Divide the topping among the sweet potato rounds.

RAW ROLL

Preparation: 5 minutes

serves 4

large handful of mustard greens or other hearty bitter greens,
    tough ends removed
zest and juice of 1 lime
30 g (1 oz) roasted salted peanuts, finely chopped
2 tablespoons pickled ginger, very finely chopped
1 cucumber

method

Toss the mustard greens with the lime juice and zest, peanuts and pickled ginger. Use a vegetable peeler to slice the cucumber into long thin strips. Very finely chop any remaining cucumber and toss with the greens. Use your hands to gather up a bite-sized amount of greens and loosely wrap in a cucumber strip. Repeat. Serve immediately.

INDEX

ACKNOWLEDGEMENTS

Thank you Catie, Kathy, Frances, Bea and Michelle for nourishing this book in all the right places.

First published by © Hachette Livre (Marabout) 2017
The English language edition published in 2018 by Hardie Grant Books,
an imprint of Hardie Grant Publishing

Hardie Grant Books (London)
5th & 6th Floors
52–54 Southwark Street
London SE1 1UN

Hardie Grant Books (Melbourne)
Building 1, 658 Church Street
Richmond, Victoria 3121

hardiegrantbooks.com

All rights reserved. No part of this publication may be reproduced, stored
in a retrieval system or transmitted in any form by any means, electronic,
mechanical, photocopying, recording or otherwise, without the prior written
permission of the publishers and copyright holders.

The moral rights of the author have been asserted.

Text © Jessica Oldfield 2018
Photography © Lauren Volvo 2018

British Library Cataloguing-in-Publication Data. A catalogue record for
this book is available from the British Library.

Vegetarian Party Food by Jessica Oldfield

ISBN 978-1-78488-185-6

Publisher: Catie Ziller
Recipes on pages 64, 76, 100, 108, 116, 128, 132, 160, 162, 164, 170, 180, 182,
184 & 188 written by Frances Boswell
Photography: Beatriz da Costa
Stylist: Frances Boswell
Designer: Alice Chadwick
Editor: Kathy Steer

For the English hardback edition:

Publisher: Kate Pollard
Publishing Assistant: Eila Purvis
Editor: Becci Wood

Colour Reproduction by p2d
Printed and bound in China by Leo Paper Group